Musa Moose

An alphabetical adventure

Waqqas Hanafi

Musa Moose – An Alphabetical Adventure
Illustrations and text copyright © 2020 Waqqas Hanafi
All rights reserved.

Musa Moose is copyright and trademark property of Waqqas Hanafi.

ISBN (paperback): 978-1-7772195-0-5
ISBN (e-book): 978-1-7772195-1-2

A is for Airplane

Musa Moose said, "See ya!"

And took an airplane to Indonesia.

Tongkonan houses of the Toraja people, South Sulawesi.

B is for Banana

Musa ate a banana; it was so yummy.

Just one big banana filled up his tummy.

Musa ingens banana with uma mbatangu houses of the Sumba people from the island of Sumba, Lesser Sunda Islands.

and C is for Chair

He sat on a chair to read a good book,
He looked around and had a good look.

Kempul and bonang gongs of the Javanese gamelan.

D is for Dragon

Musa yanked the tail of a Komodo dragon,
The dragon got mad and burned down the cabin!

Komodo Island, for which the world's largest lizard is named, East Nusa Tenggara.

and E is for Elephant

What is that on the elephant's nose?

Is it a shower or a garden hose?

Pagaruyung Palace in the Minangkabau Rumah gadang style, West Sumatra.

F is for Fish

Musa swam with the fish in the sea,
Let's count: one, two, three!

and G is for Golf

He played golf with his club and his ball,
He thought that the ball was so very small!

Prambanan Temple, Yogyakarta.

H is for House

Into the house! Quickly, get in!

Before you get caught by the chicken!

Bajau houses in Kabalutan, Togian Islands, Central Sulawesi.

and I is for Island

Let's go to an island in the sea,

An island with a flag but not a single tree.

Timang beach, Yogyakarta.

J is for Jungle

The monkeys swing from tree to tree,

And in the jungle, they roam free.

Panthera pardus melas, the Javan leopard.

and K is for Kettle

Pour some hot tea from the kettle,

Careful, it's heavy and made of metal.

A street-side angkringan with a becak pedicab passing by, Yogyakarta.

L is for Ladder

A ladder lets you climb up high,

But don't jump! You cannot fly!

A dvarapala door guardian statue, Yogyakarta.

and M is for Motorcycle

The motorcycle is much like a scooter,

And you can ride it from Calgary to Vancouver.

Provincial license plate, Yogyakarta.

N is for Nest

Some nests are way up high,

Close to where birds like to fly.

A street sign on Malioboro Street written in Javanese script, Yogyakarta.

ond O is for Omelet

The omelet smells delicious,

Cooked according to Musa's wishes.

P is for Parachute

Musa gained altitude,

Flying high using his parachute.

Bromo Tengger Semeru National Park, East Java.

and Q is for Quiet

Sometimes it's hard to be silent,

You keep laughing when you'd rather be quiet.

Melasti ceremony, several days prior to Nyepi, the Day of Silence, Bali.

R is for Rain

Where do clouds bring the rain from?

How do they know when to come?

Borobudur, the world's largest Buddhist temple, Central Java.

and S is for Shoes

Don't lose your left shoe or your right shoe,
If you lose one, you have to buy two!

Masjid Raya Al Mashun, The Great Mosque of Medan.

T is for Train

The train station is still far away,

But we are definitely headed that way.

The CC206 locomotive draped by Puncak Jaya, the summit of Mount Jayawijaya, the tallest peak in Indonesia, Papua.

and U is for Ukulele

Musa loves to play the ukulele,
Will he sing too? Maybe.

A modern dangdut performance.

V is for Volcano

That's not a dragon! It's a volcano!

We have to get out of here. Come on! Let's go!

Mount Merapi, the most active volcano in Indonesia, Yogyakarta.

and W is for Whale

Look at that great, big tail!

It certainly belongs to a big, blue whale.

Whale hunters of Lamalera, East Nusa Tenggara.

and X is for X-Ray

An x-ray is a picture of your bones,

But you can't take it with your phone.

Y is for Yoga

You can't do yoga without,

Stretching your arms and legs out.

The split gates of the outermost sanctum of Pura Penataran Agung temple with Mount Lempuyang visible behind them, Bali.

and Z is for Zombie

Zombies eat brains, we all know that,

Now, run away! What are y'all still lookin' at?!

Shirt with the emblem of Universitas Gadjah Mada, Yogyakarta.

Author

Dr Waqqas Hanafi spent a great deal of time in Indonesia, far away from his family who live in Canada. This inspired him to write an Indonesian themed alphabet book for his nephew, Musa. He bought a watercolor set and started painting. The world was suffering a coronavirus pandemic with everyone locked indoors, and Waqqas kept himself busy painting Musa Moose – a labor of love.

This book is dedicated to Mariam and Musa.

www.ingramcontent.com/pod-product-compliance
Lightning Source LLC
LaVergne TN
LVHW072116070426
835510LV00002B/81